THIS BOOK BELONGS TO:

....

....

the
52 Lists
project

the 52 lists project

A YEAR OF WEEKLY JOURNALING INSPIRATION

BY MOOREA SEAL

Illustrations by Julia Manchik
Photographs by Julia and Yuriy Manchik

SASQUATCH BOOKS
SEATTLE

Printed in China

Published by Sasquatch Books

19 18 17 16   10 9 8 7

Editor: Hannah Elnan
Production editors: Nancy W. Cortelyou and Emma Reh
Illustrations: Julia Manchik
Photographs: Julia and Yuriy Manchik
Design: Joyce Hwang

Library of Congress Cataloging-in-Publication Data
is available.

ISBN: 978-1-63217-034-7

Sasquatch Books
1904 Third Avenue, Suite 710
Seattle, WA 98101
(206) 467-4300
www.sasquatchbooks.com
custserv@sasquatchbooks.com

To my little sisters, who since their entrance into this world have inspired me to be more compassionate, to live with determination and strength, and to be more mindful of the person I am becoming everyday. By simply being, they have taught me that the best way to love others is to start by loving myself, and their fiercely loving hearts are all a big sister could ask for.

The act of list making is such an essential part of our everyday lives, whether we jot down those lists on paper or create plans in our minds. From scribbling down daily tasks, mapping out lifelong goals, or tallying up our top ten favorite songs, so many of our inner desires and thoughts are revealed through the lists we create.

I've been a serious list maker my whole life. At work I juggle three different types of lists to keep myself on track. One of the first blogs I ever published was all about listing out my favorite things, aptly called "Miss Lists." And lately, I came to the realization that list making doesn't have to be just about keeping a tally on things I need to remember or work goals I need to complete. Lists can be a tool for self-discovery, exploration, and plenty of fun too.

In this journal, you'll find ways to make each week of the year more thoughtful and vibrant by looking deeply inside of yourself to reveal your inner wisdom and confidence. To begin this journey, start with a curious spirit and get ready to discover the beauty, joy, creativity, and power that is already inside of you.

You can start the journal beginning at List 1 or jump ahead to the current season. This book is yours to make your own! Flip through the pages, feel the mood of each season, and enjoy your exploration of self. This year is already on its way to being your greatest year yet, and I couldn't feel luckier to be a part of your incredible journey.

Happy listing!

Xo Moorea Seal

Get Together

At this very moment, there is a whole community of people who are taking this same journey of self-reflection and self-discovery! Reach out and get to know them on social media by using the hashtag **#52ListsProject** when posting about your weekly list. There is so much we can learn by looking deeper inside of ourselves. And there is even more to discover when we share our common experiences and celebrate our differences as a greater community. Perhaps you will discover a few friends along the way as you share your lists via social media! You can find me on the web as well at @mooreaseal. I'm so excited to follow your journey as the seasons change.

Visit **MooreaSeal.com/pages/52Lists** to get involved!

Contents

Winter

Spring

Summer

Fall

Winter

List 1

LIST YOUR GOALS AND DREAMS
FOR THIS YEAR.

....

....

....

....

....

....

....

....

....

....

....

....

....

....

....

....

....

....

....

....

....

....

....

....

....

....

....

TAKE ACTION: What is the first step toward achieving your biggest goal? Pick one thing you can do this week to get started!

List 2

LIST YOUR FAVORITE CHARACTERS FROM BOOKS, MOVIES, ETC.

....

....

....

....

....

....

....

....

....

....

....

....

....

....

....

....

....

....

....

....

....

....

....

....

TAKE ACTION: Find a common personality trait between your favorite characters. What is one character trait that you admire in your favorite characters that you can work towards this week?

List 3

LIST THE HAPPIEST MOMENTS
OF YOUR LIFE SO FAR.

....

....

....

....

....

....

....

....

....

....

....

....

....

....

....

....

....

....

....

....

....

....

....

....

....

....

....

....

TAKE ACTION: Sometimes it's easy to forget all of the wonderful things that have happened in our lives. Come back to this list every day this week to remember: you live a beautiful life.

List 4

LIST THE SOUNDTRACK OF YOUR LIFE RIGHT NOW.

....

....

....

....

....

....

....

....

....

....

....

....

....

....

....

....

....

TAKE ACTION: Make a playlist of these songs as a memento of the person that you are at this very moment. Revisit this list in the summertime and again in the winter to see if the songs that feel like you change with the seasons.

List 5

LIST WHAT YOU WOULD LIKE
YOUR LIFE TO LOOK LIKE IN TEN YEARS.

....

....

....

....

....

....

....

....

....

....

....

....

....

....

....

....

....

....

....

....

....

....

....

....

....

....

....

....

....

....

TAKE ACTION: What are some small steps you can take right now to make one of your dreams happen in the future?

List 6

LIST THE WAYS YOU LOVE
TO HAVE FUN.

··

··

··

··

··

··

··

··

··

··

··

··

··

··

TAKE ACTION: Plan to integrate something fun into every day this week. We can all settle into routines very easily, so why not break the routine of boredom and start a routine of fun?

List 7

LIST ALL THE PEOPLE
WHO BRIGHTEN YOUR DAY.

....

....

....

....

....

....

....

....

....

....

....

....

....

....

....

....

....

....

....

....

....

....

....

....

....

....

TAKE ACTION: Write a sweet note to or do something thoughtful for one or some of these people who make your life easier, lighter, and happier.

List 8

LIST YOUR FAVORITE QUOTES.

....
....
....
....
....
....
....
....
....
....
....
....
....
....
....

....

....

....

....

....

....

....

....

....

....

....

....

....

TAKE ACTION: What do your favorite quotes have in common? Choose one quality or theme to incorporate into your daily life this week.

List 9

LIST THE THINGS YOU TREASURE MOST.

....

....

....

....

....

....

....

....

....

....

....

....

....

TAKE ACTION: How can you actively honor the things and people you love most? Spend time this week thinking of ways to surround yourself with treasured items, people, etc.

List 10

LIST THE THINGS YOU SHOULD IGNORE.

....

....

....

....

....

....

....

....

....

....

....

....

....

....

....

....

....

....

....

....

....

....

....

....

....

TAKE ACTION: Cross out all of these things and only focus on facing the challenges that make you a better version of you!

List 11

LIST THE WAYS YOU CAN
REJUVENATE YOUR SPACE.

_____

_____

_____

_____

_____

_____

_____

_____

_____

_____

_____

_____

_____

TAKE ACTION: Pick one thing you can do this week and notice how your space (and your mood) changes!

List 12

LIST YOUR BEST QUALITIES.

....

....

....

....

....

....

....

....

....

....

....

....

....

TAKE ACTION: Keep adding to this list through-out the year as you realize more and more of the unique and incredible things that make you, you. You have a lot of be proud of!

List 13

LIST THE THINGS THAT ALWAYS
CHEER YOU UP.

....

....

....

....

....

....

....

....

....

....

....

....

....

....

....

TAKE ACTION: Circle the things on your list that you can do for yourself. You are the only owner of your happiness!

Spring

List 14

LIST THE WAYS YOU CAN CLEANSE
YOUR LIFE FOR SPRING.

....

....

....

....

....

....

....

....

....

....

....

....

....

....

TAKE ACTION: Plan one way you will cleanse this week. From your space and your closet to your mind and body, there are always ways to refresh!

List 15

LIST YOUR DREAM TRIPS.

....
....
....
....
....
....
....
....
....
....
....
....
....
....

....

....

....

....

....

....

....

....

....

....

....

....

....

....

TAKE ACTION: What are the sorts of things you like to do on vacation? How can you integrate similar activities into your average week?

List 16

LIST YOUR ESSENTIALS.

....

....

....

....

....

....

....

....

....

....

....

....

....

....

TAKE ACTION: Are your essentials sentimental or practical? Take some time this week to reflect on how your essentials make you who you are.

List 17

LIST THE DIFFICULT MOMENTS IN YOUR PAST
THAT HAVE SHAPED YOU FOR THE BETTER.

....

....

....

....

....

....

....

....

....

....

....

....

....

....

TAKE ACTION: Go look in the mirror and read your list out loud. You have experienced situations that were out of your control and used your reactions to turn them into positive changes in your life. You are incredible.

List 18

LIST THE THINGS THAT MOTIVATE YOU.

....

....

....

....

....

....

....

....

....

....

....

....

....

....

....

TAKE ACTION: Practice turning one of your motivators into a daily habit that will push you to take action and make your accomplishments happen.

List 19

LIST THE PEOPLE YOU
MOST WANT TO BE LIKE.

....

....

....

....

....

....

....

....

....

....

....

....

....

....

....

....

....

....

....

....

....

....

....

....

TAKE ACTION: The world is filled with noteworthy people to look up to. Which person do you most want to emulate in your own life and how can you take action to be more like them?

List 20

LIST THE THINGS THAT
MAKE YOUR SPIRIT FEEL FREE.

....

....

....

....

....

....

....

....

....

....

....

....

....

....

....

TAKE ACTION: Turn one of your easiest freedom-enhancing activities into a weekly routine. You deserve a little magic and lightness this year.

List 21

LIST THE THINGS YOU WANT TO MAKE.

....

....

....

....

....

....

....

....

....

....

TAKE ACTION: Start one new project this week and set a date to complete it by.

List 22

LIST YOUR FAVORITE PLACES
YOU HAVE BEEN.

....

....

....

....

....

....

....

....

....

....

TAKE ACTION: What made these places so wonderful? Are there places in your community that could transport you in the same way? Schedule an outing this week that mirrors a favorite place or experience.

List 23

LIST THE THINGS THAT MAKE YOU LAUGH.

....

....

....

....

....

....

....

....

....

....

....

....

....

TAKE ACTION: This week, fill your days with actions that cause you to laugh more. Try focusing on spending time with people who always spark joy and laughter in your life.

List 24

LIST YOUR QUIRKS.

....

....

....

....

....

....

....

....

....

....

....

....

....

....

TAKE ACTION: Read your list. Did you write any in a negative way? Rewrite them from a positive perspective. Then tape them to your mirror and be reminded every day that you are quirky, charming, and wonderful.

List 25

LIST THE THINGS THAT
MAKE YOU FEEL POWERFUL.

....

....

....

....

....

....

....

....

....

....

....

....

TAKE ACTION: Make a copy of this page to keep in your wallet, so you have a daily reminder that you are strong and can face any challenge. When you have an arsenal of powerful motivators, it's easier to face challenges and kick them to the curb!

List 26

LIST THE THINGS YOU WOULD CHANGE
IN YOUR LIFE RIGHT NOW IF YOU COULD.

....

....

....

....

....

....

....

....

....

....

....

....

TAKE ACTION: Give yourself a goal this week of creating change in one small way, from changing up your bedding to re-organizing your clothing.

List 27

LIST THE THINGS THAT MAKE YOU
FEEL HEALTHY: MIND, BODY, AND SOUL.

....

....

....

....

....

....

....

....

....

....

....

....

....

TAKE ACTION: Try combining a few of your healthy habits to start this week off right.

List 28

LIST THE WILDEST THINGS
YOU WANT TO TRY.

....

....

....

....

....

....

....

....

....

....

....

....

....

....

....
....
....
....
....
....
....
....
....
....

TAKE ACTION: Do you have a bucket list? Are all of these things on it? Maybe it's about time that you got a little wild and did something outside of your norm. Go do something crazy!

List 29

LIST YOUR CHILDHOOD AND CURRENT DREAM JOBS.

List 30

LIST THE QUALITIES
YOU ADMIRE MOST IN OTHERS.

....

....

....

....

....

....

....

....

....

....

....

....

....

TAKE ACTION: Choose one of these qualities to focus on this week. Make it a goal each day to act out the quality that most inspires you.

List 31

LIST THE WORDS THAT
DEFINE YOUR PERSONALITY.

....

....

....

....

....

....

....

....

....

....

....

....

TAKE ACTION: Go through your list and see if there are any negative sounding words that you could change to be more positive. For example, "bossy" can have a negative connotation, how about changing that to "strong willed" or "in charge"? You're a boss in the best sense.

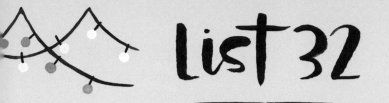

List 32

LIST THE WAYS YOU GET ENERGIZED.

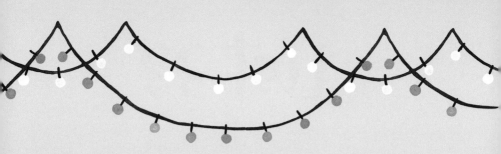

··

··

··

··

··

··

··

··

··

··

··

TAKE ACTION: This week, plan an energizing activity with one, or a group, of your favorite people! Then write down how you felt about the experience.

List 33

LIST THE WAYS THAT YOU ARE A LEADER.

....

....

....

....

....

....

....

....

....

....

....

....

....

....

TAKE ACTION: This week, practice investing more in yourself: eat a bigger healthier meal to start off the day or simply look in the mirror after you wake up or before you go to bed and say out loud "I'm a boss!" That way, when it's time for you to lead, you feel fulfilled and ready to face the challenge.

List 34

LIST THE THINGS THAT
MAKE YOU EXCITED.

TAKE ACTION: You know that feeling of butterflies in your stomach? Make it a goal this week to achieve that feeling by trying something new and exciting!

List 35

LIST THE OBSTACLES THAT STAND
IN THE WAY OF FACING YOUR DREAMS.

....

....

....

....

....

....

....

....

....

....

....

....

....

....

....

....

....

....

....

....

....

....

....

....

....

....

....

....

TAKE ACTION: Cross out all the obstacles that are outside of your control. Choose one small obstacle that is within your own power, and plan one way to start tackling it this week!

List 36

LIST EVERYTHING YOU LOVE TO DO OUTDOORS.

....

....

....

....

....

....

....

....

....

....

....

....

....

....

TAKE ACTION: This week, think of a way to bring one of your favorite indoor activities outside. Did you know that creating and engaging in new experiences is the quickest way to achieving that feeling of fulfillment and happiness?

List 37

LIST WHAT YOU WOULD SPEND
A MILLION DOLLARS ON, JUST FOR YOU.

....
....
....
....
....
....
....
....
....
....
....

TAKE ACTION: Are you surprised by anything on the list? What does your list tell you about yourself, your priorities, likes, and dislikes?

List 38

LIST THE WAYS YOU CAN LOVE YOURSELF MORE.

TAKE ACTION: Start a weekly habit that is all about self-love that you will carry out until the end of the year. Try painting your nails, going for a hike, cooking a meal from scratch, or whatever speaks to you to symbolize your personal investment.

List 39

LIST THE MOST BEAUTIFUL THINGS
YOU HAVE EVER SEEN.

....

....

....

....

....

....

....

....

....

....

....

....

....

....

....

....

....

....

....

....

....

....

....

TAKE ACTION: Without spending any money, what are a few ways you can experience more beauty in your everyday life?

List 40

LIST YOUR TOP TWENTY
MOOD-BOOSTING SONGS.

....

....

....

....

....

....

....

....

....

....

....

....

....

....

....

....

....

....

....

....

....

....

....

....

....

....

....

....

....

....

TAKE ACTION: Make this into a playlist so the next time you are feeling down, you can listen to it on repeat!

List 41

LIST ALL OF YOUR FAVORITE
THINGS ABOUT FALL.

List 42

LIST THE THINGS THAT
MAKE YOU FEEL PEACEFUL.

....

....

....

....

....

....

....

....

....

....

....

....

....

....

TAKE ACTION: This week, challenge yourself to take a few hours or a whole day completely away from technology to instead do something by yourself that makes you feel calm and at peace. Come back and write about everything that you felt and experienced.

List 43

LIST YOUR FAVORITE MEALS
AND TREATS.

....

....

....

....

....

....

....

....

....

....

....

....

TAKE ACTION: Choose a favorite treat or meal this week and share it with someone you love. Cook something for the people you love or make a date and treat someone special to a delicious meal out.

List 44

LIST THE WORDS THAT WARM YOUR SPIRIT.

List 45

LIST THE THINGS THAT MAKE UP
YOUR IDEAL HOLIDAY SEASON.

....

....

....

....

....

....

....

....

....

....

....

....

TAKE ACTION: Choose three ways that you can prep for the holidays to make this holiday season your most peace-filled, joyful, and celebratory season ever. Perhaps it is a change of attitude, finding calm amidst the bustle and hustle of the season. Or maybe it's simply planning how you will decorate your home festively!

List 46

LIST YOUR GREATEST COMFORTS.

....

....

....

....

....

....

....

....

....

....

TAKE ACTION: That feeling of comfort and warmth is such a sweet treasure. How many of your comforts can you combine into one magical and soul-filling experience? I dare you to try!